The Way We Go

Your Roadmap to a Better Future

Pat Heydlauff

The Way We Go: Your Roadmap for a Better Future
Copyright © 2017 by Pat Heydlauff

All rights reserved. No part of this book may be used or reproduced by any means, graphic, electronic, or mechanical, including photocopying, recording, taping, or by any information system without the written permission of the publisher, except in the case of brief quotations embodied in critical articles and reviews.

Energy Design books can be ordered through booksellers or by contacting:
Energy Design
561-628-3481

Cover Designer: Janet Aiossa
Editor: Dawn Josephson

ISBN: 978-0-9983347-3-8
Published by Energy Design
2017
Second Edition

First Printed 2013

Praise for *The Way We Go*

"Pat Heydlauff's book goes beyond the typical advice found in most spirituality books. By combining a unique mixture of artwork and words, it inspired me to ask questions and seek answers within. I highly recommend this book for anyone on a journey for a deeper connection."
—Pam Lontos, President, Pam Lontos Consulting, author of
I See Your Name Everywhere

"With all the technology, chaos, and stress in our daily lives, we're all seeking deeper and more meaningful connections. Pat Heydlauff's book, *The Way We Go: Your Roadmap to a Better Future*, provides a visual and verbal roadmap and inspiration."
—Jill Cook-Richards, spiritual advisor and author of
How to Heal Every Relationship in the Book from A to Z

"Pat Heydlauff—through both her art and her words—helps light the path to the personal journey so many of us talk about, but keep putting off. Pat takes both our eyes and our spirits on journeys of discovery."
—Steve Winston, President, Winston Communications

"Pat's artwork always gives me a calming feeling, and yet at the same time, an excitement that brings me to the edge of another new and uplifting promise of more to come in this life."
—Pamela Bertva, President Office Extensions

Dedication

This book is dedicated to those who have endlessly encouraged me, my creative Endeavors, and belief that everyone can create a better tomorrow.

My daughter
Lorna West

And three special friends
Pamela Bertva
Betty Humes
and
Zora Olsson

Also by Pat Heydlauff

21 Ways to Increase Employee Engagement

Feng Shui, So Easy a Child Can Do It

Selling Your Home with a Competitive Edge

Artwork available at
www.spiritualartwork.net
info@spiritualartwork.net

Contact Pat for commissioned artwork or to speak at your next event.

Contents

Introduction — ix

Awakening — 1

The Way We Go,
    Your Roadmap to a Better Future — 2

Knowing — 52

Epilogue — 55

Introduction

We all begin somewhere and perhaps unknowingly like I did. Somehow internally we know it's time—time to begin, to search for who we are, why we are here.

For me, it began when nothing seemed to be going right and everything seemed out of balance and no hope in sight. It was as if I was the right person in the wrong body at the right time but in the wrong place and didn't understand why. Have you ever felt this way? Do you feel this way now?

It was a time of transition. When I began, I was mentally still living the CEO's high stress pressure cooker world I had left four years earlier except now the stress and chaos were self-inflicted. Hope was replaced by despair, calm by chaos, and peace by fear. Unknowingly I started to balance my world by learning to paint. I painted everything from fun little decorative items to elegant home décor pieces and finally canvases. My children used to tease me, "If it doesn't move, Mom will paint it."

Painting and using the creative side of my brain became a form of prayer or meditation. It released stress, calmed my chaos, inspired me, and returned hope. It also made me feel so connected and peaceful. I fell in love with the energy of the colors, shapes, and design. They uplifted me, calmed me, and slowly brought balance and joy back into my life. It was wonderful.

Yes, it was wonderful but something was still missing. There was a hole in my heart. It was aching and longing for something—but what? I was painfully aware of this emptiness yet my mind could not grasp what was causing it. It was at this point in my life I sustained what could have been a tragic eye injury that left me with a shattered lens, a cataract, and blind in the right eye. Five surgeries later filled with much pain, many questions, and forced downtime for recovery, I can physically see again as well as see life more clearly.

During that healing time I continued my internal search and added journaling to my creative time. Finally, I began not only my road to physical recovery but also my journey within to find my deep abiding spiritual connection and joy. The hole in my heart was being nurtured and becoming whole.

A creative shift also showed up in my artwork and my canvas painting became a spiritual experience as I tuned into the energy of the colors, shapes, and design. My creativity was coming from deep within yet still connected to the outside world. At first I didn't understand it but it didn't matter. My eye and my heart were both healing and I felt joy returning to my life.

My spiritual journey took me seven years. During that time I felt hope and despair, joy and distress, anguish and contentment, chaos and calm, often failure but occasionally success. Yet never did I consider turning back or stopping. Hindsight has shown me that I actually was recording my journey through the energy of the colors, shapes, and designs on canvas as well as through words with pen and paper.

It wasn't until that portion of my journey was complete that I could look at my entire collection of artwork and realize what I had created during those sometimes joy-filled and other times anxious stress-filled times. There it was in living color, my journey—the journey of all humans traveling on the path to remember who we are and that we are eternally connected. To remember that we all need to find ways to remove chaos, fear, and despair from our lives and replace them with hope, peace, and joy. The result is balance and discovering and enjoying a deep nurturing connection with our ever-present eternal Creator.

As you read the verses and view the artwork, allow the energy of the colors, shapes, and designs to guide you to your own place of peace and calm. And, may it encourage you to search for your deep abiding connection with your Creator so you too can experience the joy.

–Pat Heydlauff

Awakening

The time for awakening and remembering
who you really are
is not only at hand
but the clock has started ticking.
God will stand at your side
and guide your every step.
Fear of failure, there is none.
You have stepped upon the path
where the light shines
and the knowing comes
and the being is.

The Way We Go

Your Roadmap to a Better Future

*Where do we begin, how do we start,
is this the way we go?*

*Should we go anywhere, should we go somewhere,
is this the way we go?*

Forgetting

When life is not going well and it seems like everything is wrong, be still and look within. Search inwardly until you find the silver thread of eternal connection guaranteed by the rainbow. Its colors are filling you with HOPE as it bathes you in PEACE and LOVE. ANGELS are guiding your way.

*Why go anywhere, why go somewhere,
would life improve?*

*Life is a stage, life is a play,
would life improve?*

Remembering

Are you traveling through life emotionally disconnected, surrounded by chaos and negativity? Find balance by remembering you are a DIVINE BEING, eternally connected to your CREATOR. You will be empowered to discover a CALM PEACE filled YOU.

*Are we the author, are we the actor,
would life improve?*

*Have we no patience, have we no tolerance,
should we change?*

Universal Connection

When you start to focus on HOPE and PEACE instead of fear and despair, you will connect both worlds — Inner and Outer. When connecting the Inner and Outer you take the FIRST step to realizing that Everyone and Everything is connected, just like planet Earth and the Universe are connected. This Universal connection is the UNLIMITED POTENTIAL that provides HOPE for a better tomorrow.

*Have we no insight, have we no understanding,
should we change?*

*Have we no lust, have we no preoccupations,
should we change?*

Soul Full

Is your Love gauge on empty? Do you feel no one cares? It just does not matter what you do, nothing goes your way? No matter how things seem, you are ALWAYS connected to the INFINITE POWER and LOVE of the UNIVERSE and its CREATOR. While on planet EARTH you are NEVER ALONE, that connection is ALWAYS there. TRUST and BELIEVE.

*Do we need to go to the end of our days
before we change?*

*Do we need to bring harm to more people
before we change?*

To Each I Give All

Without HOPE there is only heaviness, negativity and despair. But HOPE is ETERNAL. It is a seed planted within YOU and is ALWAYS connected to the Creator. All of mankind IS connected to the UNIVERSE and EACH Other. Your Silver thread of HOPE will lead you to PEACE and JOY.

*Do we need to kill more babies
before we change?*

*Do we need to accuse the accuser
before we change?*

Calming Your Chaos

Are you buried under cynicism and the hopelessness of the clutter? Is there chaos in your surroundings of people, thinking and troubles? You may have traveled this path many times but NOW is the time for escape. There is a way out. Follow that silver threaded path that is beckoning from your own Inner Spirit to the inner CALM and place of REST. From there NEW thoughts and NEW Ideas will be presented to you. Focus on your journey WITHIN and rediscover the ETERNAL connections of HOPE, INTUITIVENESS, LOVE and WISDOM.

*Do we need to look within
before we change?*

Have we given up being change?

Searching

Like an ETERNAL heartbeat, God constantly reaches out to connect to ALL seeking Beings. Your ever-present INNER knowingness affirms your connection to the INFINITE KNOWLEDGE and WISDOM proving ALL is WELL. While traveling on your PATH, your Creator is ALWAYS there. SEEK inwardly for the connection knowing that when PEACE prevails you have reached your DESTINATION.

*Are we so driven a people
that we can't accept change?*

*Are we so mired in prejudices
that we can't accept change?*

Hope

Is stress, anxiety or despair keeping you from Success, Happiness and Peace? If so quiet your mind and wrap yourself in the colors of the Rainbow, FEEL the Infinite Peace, FEEL the energy and power from the colors, FEEL the hope. Let go of the past and EMPOWER yourself in the MOMENT to CONNECT with the new better you.

*Are we so overwhelmed with tomorrow
that we can't accept change?*

*Are we so driven and involved
that we can't accept change?*

Love

Feeling unloved, disliked or singled out? Cradle yourself in the SECURITY of your Creator's eternal LOVE. Enfold yourself in the color energy of the Rainbow. You will come to realize the LOVE is always there for you at any moment. Learn that you must LOVE yourself FIRST to experience the BEAUTIFUL person that you ALREADY are. You are ONE connected with Infinite Eternal LOVE.

*Are we so void of our past
that we can't accept change?*

*Are we so afraid of tomorrow
that we can't accept change?*

Eternal Fertility

Are you thriving and blooming where you are planted? There are NO mistakes in where you are at. Your Journey, Progress and SUCCESS are waiting for your ACCEPTANCE. Your FUTURE is about staying TUNED into your GOALS. When your KNOWLEDGE within is combined with your eternal CONNECTION you will be NURTURED and GUIDED so you can CREATE the future you CHOOSE.

*Are we so afraid of God
that we can't accept change?*

*Are we so afraid of God
that we won't look within?*

The Way to Fulfillment

You may step tentatively or boldly onto you PATH to begin your journey WITHIN so you can RECOGNIZE who you are. There is a UNIVERSAL journey everyone travels. When you feel listless and a deep longing it is time to PROCEED. The Silver Thread of ETERNAL knowledge awaits YOUR arrival.

*Are we so afraid of God
that we hide from our past?*

*Are we so afraid of God
that we can't hear His voice?*

Finding Soul

Sometimes it is a PICTURE, other times a WRITTEN or SPOKEN word that helps you DISCOVER your INNER voice. Through many QUIET hours of longing and seeking you will discover your SPIRITUL Self. When absolutely QUIET and STILL, you will hear that CALM voice within and you will REJOICE in KNOWING you ARE tuned in and CONNECTED.

*Are we so afraid of God
that we look beyond Him?*

*Are we so afraid of God
that we totally ignore Him?*

Birthing Self

Discovering your INNER voice, your HIGHER SELF and your SPIRITUAL connection is very EMPOWERING and joyful. The RICH colors of birthing energy SURROUND you. Finding the DIVINE, you are filled with the EXCITEMENT and ANTICIPATION of a HOPE-filled future.

*Are we so afraid of God
that we won't begin?*

*Are we so afraid of God
that we won't take the first step?*

Gifting Energy

When you CONSCIOUSLY UNITE with your Spiritual Self you are overflowing with HOPE and LOVE. The HIGH energy colors ENCOURAGE and EMPOWER you to share your JOY with others.

*Are we so afraid of God
that we look to others?*

*Are we so afraid of God
that we ignore God's love?*

Evolving

Bathed in the colors of the RAINBOW and energy of HOPE, PEACE and JOY you EVOLVE. The cycle begins anew. The pattern of searching and growing continues as you merge into the New you. Every day you come closer to your WISHES and DREAMS.

*Are we so afraid of God
that we choose not to fly?*

*Are we so afraid of God
that we will begin to see the truth?*

Finding Inner Self

When you don't let fear and doubt get in your way you find your INNER Self and Eternal Connection. The energy of the colors, shapes and words LOVE, JOY and WISDOM lead you to find the Foundation of your SOUL Truth. When you KNOW Truth there are NO needs.

*Are we so afraid of God
that the truth is real?*

*Are we so afraid of God
that knowing the truth will set us free?*

Fertile Foundation

Once you have connected the Inner and Outer, a fertile foundation is ALWAYS available for birthing ANYTHING you choose. By eliminating turmoil and chaos, the Energy of the Rainbow is an ever PRESENT fertile foundation for bearing the fruit of SUCCESS.

*Are we so afraid of God
that knowing the Creator is love?*

*Are we so afraid of love
that we don't know which way to go?*

Ascension

Does your level of GROWTH, CALM and PEACE seem tiny at times? ACKNOWLEDGE each no matter how small and continue on your journey. Your SPIRITS will be UPLIFTED as your WISDOM and INTUITIVENESS will expand.

*God is omnipotent omniscient omnipresent
and never changes.*

*God is the truth, God is the universe
and is love, just and peace within.*

Passage

SUCCESS at last! One step at a time filled with HOPE, LOVE and KNOWLEDGE you are bathed in the colors of the rainbow showing the roadmap to your future. Success is what you find when crossing the invisible bridge of FAITH.

*How do we find God
where do we look?*

*God is by our side
and deep within our soul.*

Energy Action Plan

Remember to connect the inner and outer and create POSITIVE energy by taking ACTION. You will go nowhere unless you get connected. Eternal LOVE, Intuitiveness and WISDOM are the results. This is your personal ACTION plan for creating the LIFE you choose.

*God is the seed of hope planted within
and is always connected.*

*God is the quiet calm
that guides us through a storm.*

Joy

Your ETERNAL connection provides you the gift of JOY in your heart. Maintain a GRATITUDE attitude and bask in the sunshine of your JOY. Your creativity blooms in the joy of the moment as you are about to begin again.

*God is the miracle of a newborn baby
and the consoling grief of a lost loved one.*

*God is our tomorrow
we need to choose our days wisely.*

Peace

The road to PEACE begins when you wrap yourself in the colors of the rainbow and travel on your journey WITHIN. As your spiritual journey unfolds chaos and turmoil are but a memory replaced by CALM and PEACE. Your burdens are LIFTED, your FUTURE is filled with LIGHT.

*It is up to us
to create our future.*

*God has provided us all we need
to create the future we want.*

Growth

The CYCLE begins anew. Despair is replaced by HOPE, fear by PEACE and insecurity by EMPOWERMENT. Based on your ETERNAL connection, the searching and GROWTH continues ONE step at a time.

*We need to make our choices count
we exchange a day of our life for what we choose.*

*God has provided for all we need
to create the future we choose.*

Happiness

Like the kiss of the breeze or the warmth of the sun, HAPPINESS comes in many forms; a whisper, a hug, a tear or a smile. While it may last for only a MOMENT the JOY in its memory lasts FOREVER as does your ETERNAL connection.

*Dream big dreams, make a plan
then take action.*

*God will support our choice
to create a better we.*

###

Balanced Love

    Your eternal connection and loving yourself inside and outside is where it all BEGINS. LOVE is the invisible bond that nurtures deep meaningful relationships with yourself and others. When in BALANCE it is filled with JOY and priceless.

Knowing

*When you access your heart,
you find your soul*

*When you find your soul,
you discover your path*

*When you travel down your path,
you become connected to God
and the universe*

*Once you are connected to God
and the universe*

You find PEACE!

Flowing Through Life

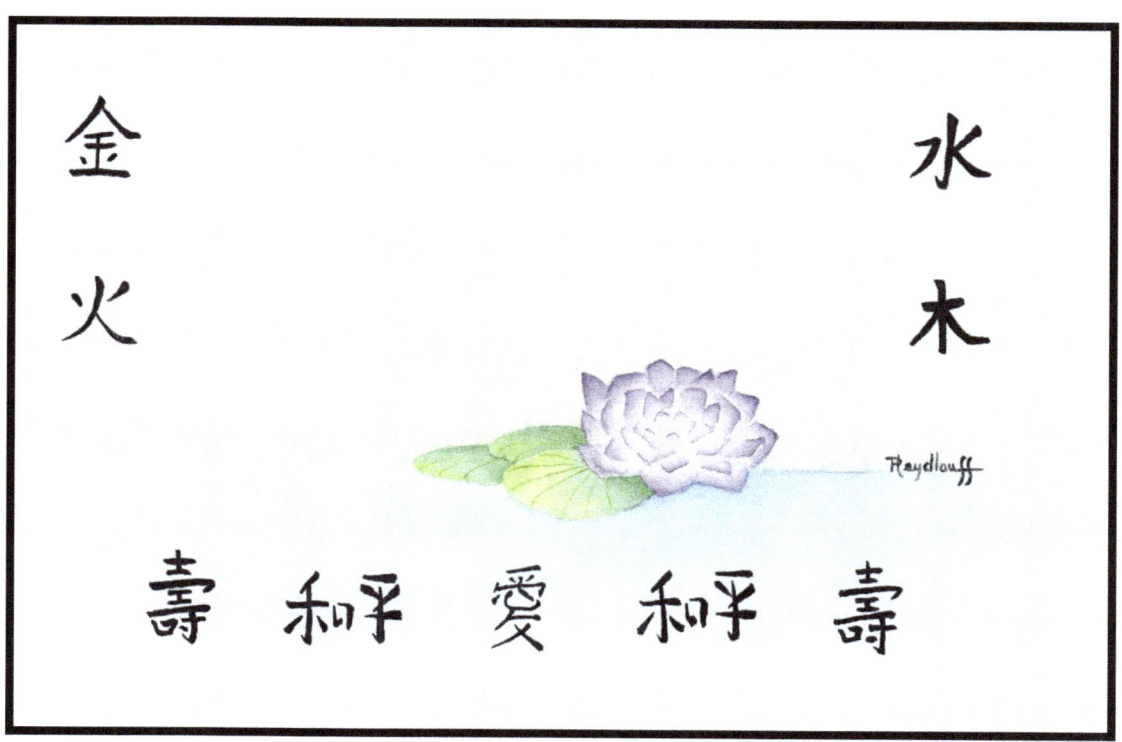

A BALANCED life that flows with PEACE and JOY is the TREASURE you find buried within. When you remove the clutter and leave the past behind, you CREATE a world of PEACE, JOY and HAPPINESS.

Epilogue

Thank you for spending this time with me. I hope the artwork, colors, and words have inspired and encouraged you to search for a better tomorrow and find peace within. Please use this book as a roadmap to encourage you along the way. Revisit the artwork and words to help reenergize and overcome the turmoil.

May you be inspired to take the first step on your journey so you can leave behind chaos and despair and discover peace and joy. The flow of life has a natural progression after you take that first step. Once you begin your journey it will take on a life of its own that is very personal, intimate, and directly yours. While journeys have similarities such as turmoil and chaos, we all experience life differently and some struggle more than others to create a better tomorrow.

It is the journey and finding your deep eternal connection that really matters, not how fast you travel or how many times you falter. When you recognize there is something more than a superficial world you are ready to find your inner voice and acknowledge the Divine.

Take your first step and seek until you find hope, unconditional love and your eternal empowering connection. You will recognize the mile markers and move forward one step at a time knowing the next step will be shown when you are ready.

Surround yourself with positive uplifting energy that is supportive and empowering. Resolve to overcome and transcend whatever you face and you will find that deep abiding connection that has always been there since the beginning of time.

Wishing you Peace and Joy Within,

Pat Heydlauff

www.ingramcontent.com/pod-product-compliance
Lightning Source LLC
Chambersburg PA
CBHW060501010526
44118CB00018B/2498